This book belongs to:

____

Made in the USA
Columbia, SC
02 June 2025

58788651R00067